D1294223

Self-

Contradictions

of the

Bible

Classics of Biblical Criticism

R. Joseph Hoffmann
Series Editor

Self-
Contradictions
of the
Bible

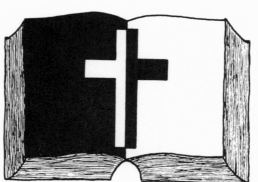

William Henry Burr

With an Introduction by R. Joseph Hoffmann

Contents

Introduction

Sometimes old diseases demand old cures. The resurgence of biblical fundamentalism in the last decade has been met on the academic side by a composed silence, bordering on *apatheia,* for which intellectuals are justly renowned. Historical certainties, in orbit around the "idea of progress," assure us that fundamentalism is not as vigorous as it seems; that its increasing control of the public's airwaves and the public's attention will, in a democracy, result in a general aversion from the ignorance and superstition that it embodies; in short, that, in an age of science and critical thinking, the fundamentalists are their own worst enemies.

There are plenty of indications to suggest that evangelists will fail to win the hearts and minds of an enlightened public. But when the scions of government offer school prayer as a remedy for the educational ills of American society—a society wherein 62 percent of Houston teachers recently failed a standard reading examination—one has reason to despair. The questions, whence literacy? and whither religion? are intimately connected.

The fact is that fundamentalism—the belief that the Bible is the inspired, inerrant, and literally true word of God—thrives on ignorance, *not* just of a general sort, but an ignorance of the Bible itself. The growth of literacy in the Western world, accompanied by the rise of democracy, was the direct result of vernacular Bible translation during the Reformation; prior to the sixteenth century, the Old and New Testaments were safely locked away in Latin, transcribed by clerics, read by (the few) competent priests, and interpreted by church scholars. It is no wonder that a text thus mystified and protected should have been an unparalleled incentive to the growth of a literate population during the process of demystification. German peasant farmers, American slaves, and country lawyers, in the simple act of learning its tropes, participated quite inadvertently in this process. Scholars during the last 100 years have participated more actively.

No process is self-sustaining. The Bible has long since been demystified, and with it has gone the incentive. Perhaps—only perhaps—this is why knowledge of the Bible has decreased dramatically in tandem with the decline in reading skills: ignorance is a great mystifier. The ability to perceive contradictions in a written text, to appreciate the nuances of historical and literary context or the intentions that ancient writers hide beneath their words are hard-acquired skills in the best of times. Fundamentalism presupposes none of them. Rather, it marks a return to the rote memorization of tropes and verses that stood at the beginning of the demystifying process. When a fundamentalist says that he "knows" the Bible, he means only that he can repeat its content selectively: he will quote Mark and John as though they were the same book; 1 Thessalonians and 2 Peter as though they were written in the same year; and, typically, the Old Testament as though it were no more than a prelude to the New. "Fundamentalism," a friend of mine is overfond of saying, "is text without context." This is self-evidently true among university students, who very often have no idea that the New Testament was written in Greek—or where—or that the term *authorized,* as applied to the 1611 version of the English Bible, refers to a British monarch's permission to publish a translation, and not to a certificate issued by God.

Even those who oppose the outdated world view of the fundamentalists are scarcely equipped to meet the enemy on his own ground: they are unable to counter the evangelical's tenets, because they, too, stand at the end of the process of demystification. Disinterest, stemming from the belief that fundamentalism is a harmless Georgia philosophy that got itself dis-elected with Jimmy Carter, or an unspoken Episcopalian conviction that the evangelicals are not to be a major influence, because they are not the right kind of people, masks the fact that the army of the reasonable—religious moderates, liberals, and skeptics—have forsaken the Bible altogether, or rather surrendered it to the other side. There will always be a feeling in enlightened circles that religion should not be a topic of conversation at the dinner table and that it is impolite to say grace when one has guests. We can only guess at what will happen when the enlightened minority recognizes that it is precisely disinterest and politeness that are threatened by the majoritarians; that quietism and freedom of conscience do not exist in their lexicon; that they are convinced that the way things are done in the Back Bay or taught at the university are in serious need of reform if American society is to rediscover its Christian past.

Fundamentalism grows because, to paraphrase Mark Twain, it is the nature of a weed to grow and because we are hard-pressed for gardeners. The escape into unreason and superstition, nurtured by widespread ignorance of history, comparative religions, and literary art, has few opponents, few who are willing to go on record as calling a weed a weed so long as weeds can vote.

This brings us roundabout to the "old Cure." In the pages that follow we have what amounts to an ingenious response to fundamentalism. Compiled in 1859 by William Henry Burr and published anonymously, *Self-Contradictions of the Bible* was described by the evangelical magazine *The World* as "a vilely composed and wretchedly printed attempt to destroy the faith of the civilized world in the Christian Religion." In fact, the pamphlet made rather more modest inroads and went out of print in 1890, fully thirty years before the now-famous Scopes trial. Burr, himself a dedicated follower of Darwin, was a newspaper reporter and, as the selection of material shows, only an amateur in the field of biblical scholarship. Some of the contradictions he points us to are indeed "palpable" (e.g., James 1.17 versus Genesis 6.6), others less so (1 Timothy 6.16 versus Psalms 97.2). But the author's failure to invoke context or linguistic usage to explain away any of the contradictions is precisely what made the pamphlet the threat that it was. Burr answered text with text, proposition with proposition, and doctrine with doctrine in a way (i.e., without comment) that infuriated his evangelical opponents.

Self-Contradictions of the Bible was hailed by the liberal journal *Banner of Light* as "the Bible subverting itself," and the pro-Darwin *Herald of Progress* declared:

> Reader: if in endeavoring to defend the truth from the flippant sallies of some disciple of orthodoxy you have at times wanted at your command the means of meeting your opponent with his own weapons and upon his own ground, let us command you to arm yourself at once with this breastplate of defense. Put it in the hands of your adversary, and if he will not receive it, read a few selections from it to him. He cannot resist its effects.

In the confidence that there are many today who prefer their meals without preface and their schooldays without prayer, I have asked Dr. Paul Kurtz, editor-in-chief of Prometheus Books, to reproduce this work in its unrevised 1860 format. At worst, I hasten to say, it is a lazy man's guide to the problems of biblical text. At best, it is a minor classic of nineteenth-century religious liberation. In either case, it may open a few eyes and quicken a few pulses, just as it did 123 years ago.

R. Joseph Hoffman
Hartwick College, Oneonta, New York

THEOLOGICAL DOCTRINES

1.

GOD IS SATISFIED WITH HIS WORKS.

And God saw everything that he had made, and behold it was *very good.* (Gen. 1 : 31.)

GOD IS **DISSATISFIED** WITH HIS WORKS.

And it *repented* the Lord that he had *made man* on the earth, and it *grieved* him at his heart. (Gen. 6 : 6.)

2.

GOD DWELLS IN CHOSEN TEMPLES.

And the Lord appeared to Solomon by night, and said unto him: I have heard thy prayer, and have chosen *this place* to myself for a *house* of sacrifice. . . . For now have I chosen and sanctified *this house,* that my name may be there forever; and mine eyes and my heart shall be *there perpetually.* (2 Chron. 7 : 12, 16.)

GOD DWELLS **NOT** IN TEMPLES.

Howbeit the Most High *dwelleth not in temples* made with hands. (Acts 7 : 48.)

3.

GOD DWELLS IN LIGHT.

Dwelling in *light* which no man can approach unto. (1 Tim. 6 : 16.)

GOD DWELLS IN **DARKNESS.**

The Lord said he would dwell in thick *darkness.* (1 Kings 8 : 12.)

He made *darkness* his secret place. (Ps. 18 : 11.)

Clouds and *darkness* are round about him. (Ps. 97 : 2.)

4.

GOD IS SEEN AND HEARD.

And I will take away my hand, and thou shalt *see* my backparts. (Ex. 33 : 23.)

And the Lord *spake* to Moses *face to face,* as a man speaketh to his friend. (Ex. 33 : 11.)

And the Lord *called* unto Adam, and said unto him, Where art thou? And he said, I *heard* thy *voice* in the garden, and I was afraid. (Gen. 3 : 9, 10.)

For I have *seen* God *face to face,* and my life is preserved. (Gen. 32 : 30.)

In the year that King Uzziah died, I *saw,* also, the Lord sitting upon a throne, high and lifted up. (Is. 6 : 1.)

Then went up Moses and Aaron, Nadab and Abihu, and seventy of the elders of Israel. And they *saw* the God of Israel. . . . They *saw* God, and did eat and drink. (Ex. 24 : 9, 10, 11.)

GOD IS **INVISIBLE** AND **CANNOT** BE HEARD.

No man hath *seen* God at any time. (John 1 : 18.)

Ye hath *neither heard* his *voice,* at any time, *nor seen* his *shape.* (John 5 : 37.)

And he said, Thou *canst not see* my face; for there shall *no* man *see* me and live. (Ex. 33 : 20.)

Whom *no* man hath *seen nor can see.* (1 Tim. 6 : 16.)

5.

GOD IS TIRED AND RESTS.

For in six days the Lord made heaven and earth, and on the seventh day he *rested,* and was *refreshed.* (Ex. 31 : 17.)

I am *weary* with repenting. (Jer. 15 : 6.)

GOD IS **NEVER** TIRED AND **NEVER** RESTS.

Hast thou not heard that the everlasting God, the Lord, the Creator of the ends of the earth, *fainteth not,* neither is *weary?* (Is. 40 : 28.)

6.

GOD IS EVERYWHERE PRESENT, SEES AND KNOWS ALL THINGS.

The eyes of the Lord are in *every place.* (Prov. 15 : 3.)

Whither shall I flee from thy *presence?* If I ascend up into heaven, thou art *there;* if I make my bed in hell, behold, thou art *there.* If I take the wings of the morning, and dwell in the uttermost parts of the sea; even *there* shall thy hand lead me, and thy right hand shall hold me. (Ps. 139 : 7-10.)

There is no darkness nor shadow of death, where the workers of iniquity may *hide* themselves. For his *eyes* are upon the *ways* of man, and he *seeth all his goings.* (Job 34 : 22, 21.)

GOD IS **NOT** EVERYWHERE PRESENT, **NEITHER** SEES **NOR** KNOWS ALL THINGS.

And the Lord *came down to see* the city and the town. (Gen. 11 : 5.)

And the Lord said, Because the cry of Sodom and Gomorrah is great, and because their sin is very grievous, I will *go down* now and *see* whether they have done altogether according to the cry of it, which is come unto me; and, *if not,* I will know. (Gen. 18 : 20, 21.)

And Adam and his wife *hid* themselves from the *presence of the Lord,* amongst the trees of the garden. (Gen. 3 : 8.)

7.

GOD KNOWS THE HEARTS OF MEN.

Thou, Lord, which *knowest the hearts of all men.* (Acts 1 : 24.)

Thou knowest my down-sitting and mine up-rising; thou understandest my thought afar off. Thou compassest my path and my lying down, and art *acquainted with all my ways.* (Ps. 139 : 2, 3.)

GOD TRIES MEN TO **FIND OUT** WHAT IS IN THEIR HEARTS.

The Lord, your God, *proveth you, to know whether* ye love the Lord, your God, with all your heart and with all your soul. (Deut. 13 : 3.)

The Lord thy God led thee these forty years in the wilderness, to humble thee, and to *prove thee, to know what was in thy heart.* (Deut. 8 : 2.)

For *now I know* that thou fearest God, seeing that thou *hast not withheld thy son,* thine only son, from me. (Gen. 22 : 12.)

8.

GOD IS ALL-POWERFUL.

Behold, I am the Lord, the God of all flesh; is there *anything too hard* for me? (Jer. 32 : 27.)

With God *all* things are *possible.* (Matt. 19 : 26.)

GOD IS **NOT** ALL-POWERFUL.

And the Lord was with Judah, and he drave out the inhabitants of the mountain; but *could not drive out* the inhabitants of the valley, because they had chariots of iron. (Judg. 1 : 19.)

9.

GOD IS UNCHANGEABLE.

With whom is no *variableness, neither shadow of turning.* (James 1: 17.)

For I am the Lord; I change not. (Mal. 3 : 6.)

I, the Lord, have spoken it; it shall come to pass, and I *will do it.* I will *not go back,* neither will I spare, neither will I *repent.* (Ezek. 24 : 14.)

God is not a man, that he should lie; neither the son of man, that he should *repent.* (Num. 23 : 19.)

GOD IS **CHANGEABLE.**

And it *repented* the Lord that he had made man on the earth, and it *grieved* him at his heart. (Gen. 6 : 6.)

And God saw their works, that they turned from their evil way; and God *repented* of the evil that he had said he *would do* unto them, and he *did it not.* (Jonah 3 : 10.)

Wherefore the Lord God of Israel saith, I said, indeed, that thy house, and the house of thy father, should walk before me forever; but now the Lord saith, *Be it far from me.* . . . Behold, the days come that I will *cut off* thine arm, and the arm of thy father's house. (1 Sam. 2 : 30, 31.)

In those days was Hezekiah sick unto death. And the prophet Isaiah, the son of Amoz, came unto him, and said unto him, Thus saith the Lord, set thy house in order; for thou *shalt die,* and not live. . . . And it came to pass afore Isaiah was gone out into the middle court, that the word of the Lord came unto him, saying, Turn again and tell Hezekiah, the captain of my people, thus saith the Lord, ... I have heard thy prayer, . . . and I will *add* unto thy days, *fifteen years.* (2 Kings 20 : 1, 4, 5, 6.)

And the Lord said unto Moses, Depart and go up hence, thou and the people. . . . For I will *not go up* in the midst of thee. . . . And the Lord said, I will do this thing, also, that thou hast spoken. . . . *My presence shall go with thee,* and I will give thee rest. (Ex. 33 : 1, 3, 17, 14.)

10.

GOD IS JUST AND IMPARTIAL.

The Lord is *upright,* . . . and there is *no unrighteousness* in him. (Ps. 92 : 15.)

Shall not the Judge of all the earth *do right?* (Gen. 18 : 25.)

A God of truth, and without iniquity, *just* and *right* is he. (Deut. 32 : 4.)

There is *no respect of persons* with God. (Rom. 2 : 11.)

Ye say the way of the Lord is not *equal.* Hear now, O house of Israel; is not my way *equal?* (Ezek. 18 : 25.)

GOD IS **UNJUST** AND **PARTIAL.**

Cursed be Canaan; a *servant of servants* shall he be unto his brethren. (Gen. 9 : 25.)

For I, the Lord thy God, am a *jealous* God, visiting the iniquity of the *fathers* upon the *children* unto the *third and fourth generation.* (Ex. 20 : 5.)

For the children being *not yet born, neither having done any good or evil,* that the purpose of God, according to election, might stand, . . . it was said unto her, The *elder shall serve the younger.* As it is written, Jacob have I *loved,* and Esau have I *hated.* (Rom. 9 : 11, 12, 13.)

For whosoever *hath,* to him shall be *given,* and he shall have *more abundance;* but whosoever *hath not,* from him shall be *taken away* even *that he hath.* (Matt. 13 : 12.)

11.

GOD IS THE AUTHOR OF EVIL.

Out of the mouth of the Most High proceedeth not *evil* and good? (Lam. 3 : 38.)

Thus saith the Lord, Behold I *frame evil* against you and *devise a device* against you. (Jer. 18 : 11.)

I make peace and *create evil.* I the Lord *do all* these things. (Is. 45 : 7.)

Shall there be *evil* in the city, and the *Lord* hath not done it? (Amos 3 : 6.)

Wherefore I gave them also *statutes that were not good,* and judgments that they *should not live.* (Ezek. 20 : 25.)

GOD IS **NOT** THE AUTHOR OF EVIL.

God is not the author of *confusion.* (1 Cor. 14 : 33.)

A God of *truth and without iniquity, just and right* is he. (Deut. 32 : 4.)

For God cannot be tempted with evil, neither *tempteth* he any man. (James 1 : 13.)

12.

GOD GIVES FREELY TO THOSE WHO ASK.

If any of you lack wisdom, let him ask of God, *that giveth to all men freely* and upbraideth not, and it shall be *given* unto him. (James 1 : 5.)

For *every* one that *asketh receiveth* and he that *seeketh findeth.* (Luke 11 : 10.)

GOD **WITHHOLDS** HIS BLESSINGS AND PREVENTS MEN FROM RECEIVING THEM.

He hath *blinded their eyes and hardened their heart* that they *should not see* with their eyes, nor *understand* with their heart, and be converted, and I should heal them. (John 12 : 40.)

For it was of the Lord to *harden their hearts,* that they should come against Israel in battle, that he might destroy them utterly, and that they might have *no favor.* (Josh. 11 : 20.)

O Lord, why hast thou made us to *err* from thy ways and *hardened our heart?* (Is. 63 : 17.)

13.

GOD IS TO BE FOUND BY THOSE WHO SEEK HIM.

Everyone that asketh receiveth, and he that *seeketh*

findeth. (Matt. 7 : 8.)

Those that *seek me early shall find me.* (Prov. 8 : 17.)

GOD IS **NOT** TO BE FOUND BY THOSE WHO SEEK HIM.

Then shall they call upon me but I will *not answer;* they shall *seek me early* but shall *not find me.* (Prov. 1 : 28.)

14.

GOD IS WARLIKE.

The Lord is a man of *war.* (Ex. 15 : 3.)
The Lord of *Hosts* is his name. (Is. 51 : 15.)

GOD IS **PEACEFUL**

The God of *peace.* (Rom. 15 : 33.)
God is not the author of confusion but of *peace.* (1 Cor. 14 : 33.)

15.

GOD IS CRUEL, UNMERCIFUL, DESTRUCTIVE, AND FEROCIOUS.

I *will not pity,* nor *spare,* nor *have mercy,* but *destroy.* (Jer. 13 : 14.)

And thou shalt *consume all the people* which the Lord thy God shall deliver thee; thine eye shall have *no pity* upon them. (Deut. 7 : 16.)

Now go and smite Amalek, and utterly destroy all that they have, and spare them not, but slay both *man and woman, infant and suckling.* (1 Sam. 15 : 2, 3.)

Because they had looked into the ark of the Lord, even

he *smote of the people fifty thousand, and three score and ten men.* (1 Sam. 6 : 19.)

The Lord thy God is a *consuming fire.* (Deut. 4 : 24.)

GOD IS **KIND, MERCIFUL,** AND **GOOD.**

The Lord is *very pitiful* and of *tender mercy.* (James 5 : 11.)

For he doth *not afflict willingly,* nor *grieve* the children of men. (Lam. 3 : 33.)

For his mercy *endureth forever.* (1 Chron. 16 : 34.)

I have no *pleasure* in the death of him that dieth, saith the Lord God. (Ezek. 18 : 32.)

The Lord is *good to all,* and his tender mercies are over *all his works.* (Ps. 145 : 9.)

Who will have *all men to be saved,* and to come unto the knowledge of the truth. (1 Tim. 2 : 4.)

God is *love.* (1 John 4 : 16.)

Good and upright is the Lord. (Ps. 25 : 8.)

16.

GOD'S ANGER IS FIERCE AND ENDURES LONG.

And the Lord's *anger was kindled* against Israel, and he made them wander in the wilderness *forty years* until *all the generation* that had done evil in the sight of the Lord was *consumed.* (Num. 32 : 13.)

And the Lord said unto Moses, Take all the heads of the people and hang them up before the Lord against the sun, that the *fierce anger* of the Lord may be turned away from Israel. (Num. 25 : 4.)

For I have kindled a fire in mine anger which shall *burn forever.* (Jer. 17 : 4.)

GOD'S ANGER IS **SLOW** AND ENDURES BUT FOR A **MOMENT.**

The Lord is merciful and gracious, *slow to anger* and plenteous in mercy. (Ps. 103 : 8.)

His anger *endureth but a moment.* (Ps. 30 : 5.)

17.

GOD COMMANDS, APPROVES OF AND DELIGHTS IN BURNT OFFERINGS, SACRIFICES, AND HOLY DAYS.

Thou shalt offer every day a *bullock* for a sin offering for atonement. (Ex. 29 : 36.)

On the tenth day of this seventh month, there shall be a *day of atonement;* it shall be a *holy convocation* unto you, and ye shall afflict your souls and offer an *offering made by fire* unto the Lord. (Lev. 23 : 27.)

And thou shalt burn the whole *ram* upon the *altar;* . . . *it is a sweet savor;* an offering made by fire unto the Lord. (Ex. 29 : 18.)

And the priest shall burn it all on the altar to be a *burnt sacrifice,* an offering made by fire, of a *sweet savor* unto the Lord. (Lev. 1 : 9.)

GOD **DISAPPROVES** OF, AND **HAS NO PLEASURE** IN BURNT OFFERINGS, SACRIFICES, AND HOLY DAYS.

For I *spake not* unto your fathers, nor commanded them in the day that I brought them out of the land of Egypt, concerning *burnt offerings* or *sacrifices.* (Jer. 7 : 22.)

Your burnt offerings are *not acceptable, nor your sacrifices sweet* unto me. (Jer. 6 : 20.)

Will I eat of the flesh of *bulls,* or drink the blood of *goats?* Offer unto God *thanksgiving,* and pay thy *vows* unto the Most high. (Ps. 50 : 13, 14.)

Bring no more *vain oblations; incense* is an *abomination* unto me; the *new moons* and *sabbaths,* the calling of *assemblies I cannot away with;* it is *iniquity,* even the *solemn meeting.* . . . To what purpose is the multitude of your *sacrifices* unto me? saith the Lord. I am full of the burnt offerings of rams, and the fat of fed beasts, and I *delight not* in the blood of bullocks, or of lambs, or of he goats. When ye come to appear before me, *who hath required this* at your hand. (Is. 1 : 13, 11, 12.)

18.

GOD ACCEPTS HUMAN SACRIFICES.

The king [David] took the two sons of Rizpah, . . . and the five sons of Michal; . . . and he delivered them into the hands of the Gibeonites, and they *hanged* them in the hill *before the Lord.* . . . And after that *God was entreated* for the land. (2 Sam. 21 : 8, 9, 14.)

And he [God] said, Take now thy son, thine only son Isaac, whom thou lovest, and get thee into the land of Moriah, and *offer* him there for a *burnt offering.* (Gen. 22 : 2.)

And Jephthah vowed a *vow* unto the *Lord,* and said, If thou shalt without fail deliver the children of Ammon into my hands, then it shall be, that whosoever cometh forth of the doors of my house to meet me when I return in peace from the children of Ammon, shall surely be the Lord's, and I will offer it up for a *burnt offering.* So Jephthah passed over unto the children of Ammon to fight against them; and the Lord delivered them into his hands. . . . And Jephthah came to Mizpeh unto his house and behold, his daughter came out to meet him. . . . And he sent her away for two months; and she went with her companions and bewailed her virginity upon the mountains. And it came to pass at the end of two months that she returned unto her father, who *did according to his vow* which he had made. (Judg. 11 : 30, 31, 32, 34, 38, 39.)

GOD **FORBIDS** HUMAN SACRIFICE.

Take heed to thyself that thou be not snared by following them [the Gentile nations]; . . . for every abomination to
the Lord which he hateth have they done unto their gods;
for even their *sons* and their *daughters* have they *burnt in
the fire to their gods.* (Deut. 12 : 30, 31.)

19.

GOD TEMPTS MEN.

And it came to pass after these things, that God did
tempt Abraham. (Gen. 22 : 1.)

And again the anger of the Lord was kindled against
Israel and *he moved* David against them to say, Go number
Israel and Judah. (2 Sam. 24 : 1.)

O Lord, thou has *deceived* [marginal reading, *enticed*]
me, and I was deceived [enticed]. (Jer. 20 : 7.)

Lead us not into *temptation.* (Matt. 6 : 13.)

GOD TEMPTS **NO** MAN.

Let no may say when he is tempted, I am *tempted of
God;* for God cannot be tempted with evil, *neither tempteth
he any man.* (James 1 : 13.)

20.

GOD CANNOT LIE.

It is impossible for God to *lie.* (Heb. 6 : 18.)

GOD **LIES BY PROXY;** HE SENDS FORTH **LYING SPIRITS** TO DECEIVE.

For this cause God shall *send them strong delusion, that they should believe a lie.* (2 Thes. 2 : 11.)

Now, therefore, behold, the Lord hath *put a lying spirit* in the mouth of all these thy prophets, and the Lord hath *spoken evil* concerning thee. (1 Kings 22 : 23.)

And if the prophet be deceived when he hath spoken a thing, I the Lord *have deceived* that prophet. (Ezek. 14 : 9).

21.

BECAUSE OF MAN'S WICKEDNESS GOD DESTROYS HIM.

And God saw that the *wickedness* of man was *great* in the earth, and that every *imagination of the thoughts of his heart was only evil continually.* . . . And the Lord said, I will *destroy* man whom I have created. (Gen. 6 : 5, 7.)

BECAUSE OF MAN'S WICKEDNESS GOD WILL **NOT** DESTROY HIM.

And the Lord said in his heart, I *will not again* curse the ground any more for man's sake; for the *imagination of man's heart is evil from his youth; neither will I smite any more every living thing.* (Gen. 8 : 21.)

22.

GOD'S ATTRIBUTES ARE REVEALED IN HIS WORKS.

For the *invisible things* of him from the creation of the world are *clearly seen,* being understood by the *things that are made,* even his *eternal power and Godhead.* (Rom. 1 : 20.)

GOD'S ATTRIBUTES **CANNOT BE DISCOVERED.**

Canst thou by searching *find out* God? (Job 11 : 7.)
There is *no searching his understanding.* (Is. 40 : 28.)

23.

THERE IS BUT ONE GOD.

The Lord our God is *one* Lord. (Deut. 6 : 4.)

THERE IS A **PLURALITY** OF GODS.

And God said, Let *us* make man in *our* image. (Gen. 1 : 26.)

And the Lord God said, Behold the man is become as one of us. (Gen. 3 : 22.)

And the Lord appeared unto him [Abraham] in the plains of Mamre. . . . And he lifted up his eyes and looked, and lo, *three men* stood by him; and when he saw them he ran to meet them from the tent door, and bowed himself toward the ground, and said, *My Lord,* if now I have found favor in thy sight, pass not away, I pray thee, from thy servant. (Gen. 18 : 1, 2, 3.)

For there are *three* that bear record in Heaven, the Father, the Word, and the Holy Ghost. (1 John 5 : 7.)

MORAL PRECEPTS

24.

ROBBERY COMMANDED.

When ye go, ye shall not go empty; but every woman shall *borrow* of her neighbor, and of her that sojourneth in her house, jewels of silver, and jewels of gold, and raiment; and ye shall put them upon your sons, and upon your daughters; and ye shall *spoil the Egyptians*. (Ex. 3 : 21, 22.)

And they *borrowed of the Egyptians* jewels of silver, and jewels of gold, and raiment. . . . And they *spoiled* the Egyptians. (Ex. 12 : 35, 36).

ROBBERY **FORBIDDEN.**

Thou shalt not defraud thy neighbor, *neither rob* him. (Lev. 19 : 13.)

Thou *shalt not steal*. (Ex. 20 : 15.)

25.

LYING APPROVED AND SANCTIONED.

And the woman [Rahab] took the two men and hid them and said thus: There came men unto me, but I wist not whence they were; and it came to pass about the time of shutting of the gate, when it was dark that *the men went out; whither the men went I wot not;* pursue after them quickly, for ye shall overtake them. But she had brought them up to the *roof of the house and hid them with the*

31

stalks of flax. (Josh. 2 : 4, 5, 6.)

Was not Rahab, the harlot, *justified* by works, when she had received the messengers, and had sent them out another way? (James 2 : 25.)

And the king of Egypt called for the midwives, and said unto them, Why have ye done this thing, and have saved the men-children alive? And the midwives said unto Pharaoh, Because *the Hebrew women are not as the Egyptian women;* for they are lively, and are *delivered ere the midwives come in unto them. Therefore God dealt well* with the midwives. (Ex. 1: 18–20.)

And there came forth a spirit, and stood before the Lord, and said, I will persuade him. . . . I will go forth and be a *lying spirit* in the mouth of all his prophets. And he said, *Thou shalt persuade him* and prevail also; *go forth and do so.* (1 Kings 22 : 21, 22.)

LYING **FORBIDDEN.**

Thou *shalt not bear false witness.* (Ex. 20 : 16.)

Lying lips are an *abomination* to the Lord. (Prov. 12 : 22.)

All *liars* shall have their part in the *lake which burneth with fire and brimstone.* (Rev. 21 : 8.)

26.

HATRED TO THE EDOMITE SANCTIONED.

He [Amaziah] slew of Edom, in the valley of Salt, ten thousand . . . And he did that which was *right* in the sight of the *Lord.* (2 Kings 14 : 7, 3.)

HATRED TO THE EDOMITE **FORBIDDEN.**

Thou shalt *not abhor* an Edomite, for he is thy *brother.* (Deut. 23 : 7.)

27.

KILLING COMMANDED.

Thus saith the Lord God of Israel, Put every man his sword by his side, and go in and out from gate to gate throughout the camp, and *slay every man his brother,* and every man his *companion,* and every man his *neighbor.* (Ex. 32 : 27.)

KILLING **FORBIDDEN.**

Thou *shalt not kill.* (Ex. 20 : 13.)

28.

THE BLOOD-SHEDDER MUST DIE.

At the hand of every man's brother will I require the *life* of man. Whoso sheddeth man's blood, by man shall his *blood* be *shed.* (Gen. 9 : 5, 6.)

THE BLOOD-SHEDDER MUST **NOT** DIE.

And the Lord set a mark upon Cain, *lest* any finding him should *kill* him. (Gen. 4 : 15.)

29.

THE MAKING OF IMAGES FORBIDDEN.

Thou shalt *not* make unto thee any graven *image,* or any *likeness* of *anything* that is in heaven above, or that is in the earth beneath. (Ex. 20 : 4.)

THE MAKING OF IMAGES **COMMANDED.**

Thou shalt make two *cherubims* of gold. . . . And the cherubims shall stretch forth their wings on high, covering the mercy seat with their wings, and their faces shall look to one another. (Ex. 25 : 18, 20.)

30.

SLAVERY AND OPPRESSION ORDAINED.

Cursed by Canaan; a *servant of servants* shall he be unto his brethren. (Gen. 9 : 25.)

Of the children of the strangers that do sojourn among you, of them shall ye *buy.* . . . They shall be your *bondmen forever;* but over your brethren of the children of Israel, ye shall not *rule with rigor.* (Lev. 25 : 45, 46.)

I will *sell* your sons and daughters into the hands of the children of Judah, and they shall *sell* them to the Sabeans, to a people afar off; for the *Lord* hath spoken it. (Joel 3 : 8.)

SLAVERY AND OPPRESSION **FORBIDDEN.**

Undo the heavy burdens . . . let the oppressed go free, . . . *break every yoke.* (Is. 58 : 6.)

Thou shalt *neither vex* a stranger, *nor oppress him.* (Ex. 22 : 21.)

He that *stealeth a man,* and *selleth him,* or if he be *found* in his *hand,* he shall surely be put to death. (Ex. 21 : 16.)

Neither be ye called *masters.* (Matt. 23 : 10.)

31.

IMPROVIDENCE ENJOINED.

Consider the *lilies* of the field, how they grow; they *toil not,* neither do they *spin.* . . . If God so *clothe the grass* of the field . . . shall he not much more *clothe you?* . . . Therefore, *take no thought,* saying, what shall we *eat?* or What shall we *drink?* or Wherewithal shall we be *clothed?* . . . Take no thought for the morrow. (Matt. 6 : 28, 31, 34.)

Give to every man that asketh of thee, and of him that taketh away thy goods, *ask them not again.* . . . And *lend,* hoping for *nothing again,* and your reward shall be great. (Luke 6 : 30, 35.)

Sell that ye have and give *alms.* (Luke 12 : 3.)

IMPROVIDENCE **CONDEMNED.**

But if any *provide not for his own,* and especially for those of his *own house,* he hath denied the faith, and is *worse than an infidel.* (1 Tim. 5 : 8.)

A *good* man leaveth an *inheritance* to his childrens' children. (Prov. 13 : 22.)

32.

ANGER APPROVED.

Be ye angry and sin not. (Eph. 4 : 26.)

ANGER **DISAPPROVED.**

Be not hasty in thy spirit to be angry; for *anger resteth in the bosom of fools.* (Eccl. 7 : 9.)

Make no friendship with an *angry* man. (Prov. 22 : 24.)

The wrath of man worketh *not* the righteousness of God. (James 1 : 20.)

33.

GOOD WORKS TO BE SEEN OF MEN.

Let your light so shine *before men,* that they may *see* your *good* works. (Matt. 5 : 16.)

GOOD WORKS **NOT** TO BE SEEN OF MEN.

Take heed that ye do not *your* alms *before men,* to be *seen* of them. (Matt. 6 : 1.)

34.

JUDGING OF OTHERS FORBIDDEN.

Judge not, that ye be not judged. For with what judgment ye judge, ye shall be judged. (Matt. 7 : 1, 2.)

JUDGING OF OTHERS **APPROVED.**

Do ye not know that the saints shall *judge the world?* And if the world shall be judged by you, are ye unworthy to judge the smallest matters? Know ye not that we shall *judge angels?* How much more things that pertain to *this life?* If, then, ye have judgments of things pertaining to this life, *set them to judge* who are least esteemed in the church. (1 Cor. 6 : 2, 3, 4.)

Do not *ye judge* them that are within? (1 Cor. 5 : 12.)

35.

CHRIST TAUGHT NONRESISTANCE.

Resist not evil, but whosoever shall *smite* thee on thy right cheek, *turn to him the other also.* (Matt. 5 : 39.)

All they that take the *sword* shall *perish* with the sword. (Matt. 26 : 52.)

CHRIST TAUGHT AND PRACTICED
PHYSICAL RESISTANCE.

He that hath no *sword,* let him sell his garment and *buy one.* (Luke 22 : 36.)

And when he had made a *scourge* of small cords, he *drove* them all out of the temple. (John 2 : 15.)

36.

CHRIST WARNED HIS FOLLOWERS NOT
TO FEAR BEING KILLED.

Be *not afraid* of them that *kill* the body. (Luke 12 : 4.)

CHRIST HIMSELF AVOIDED THE JEWS
FOR **FEAR** OF BEING KILLED.

After these things Jesus walked in Galilee; for he would *not* walk in Jewry, because the Jews sought to *kill* him. (John 7 : 1.)

37.

PUBLIC PRAYER SANCTIONED.

And Solomon stood before the altar of the Lord in the presence of *all the congregation* of Israel, and spread forth his hands toward heaven. [Then follows the prayer.] And it was so, that when Solomon had made an end of praying all this *prayer and supplication* unto the Lord, he arose from before the altar of the Lord, from kneeling on his knees, with his hands spread up to heaven. . . . And the Lord said unto him, I have *heard* thy prayer and thy supplication that thou hast made before me. (1 Kings 8 : 22, 54; & 9 : 3.)

PUBLIC PRAYER **DISAPPROVED.**

When thou prayest thou shalt not be as the hypocrites are; for they love to pray *standing in the synagogues* and in the corners of the streets, that they may be *seen of men.* . . . But thou, when thou prayest, enter into thy *closet,* and when thou hast *shut thy door,* pray to thy Father which is in *secret.* (Matt. 6 : 5, 6.)

38.

IMPORTUNITY IN PRAYER COMMENDED.

Because this widow troubleth me, I will avenge her, lest by her *continual* coming she *weary* me. . . . And shall not God avenge his own elect, which cry *day* and *night* unto him? (Luke 18 : 5, 7.)

Because of his *importunity* he will rise and give him as many as he needeth. (Luke 11 : 8.)

IMPORTUNITY IN PRAYER **CONDEMNED.**

But when ye pray, use not vain repetitions as the heathen do; for they think that they shall be heard for their *much speaking.* Be ye *not* therefore like unto them; for your Father knoweth what things ye have need of before ye ask him. (Matt. 6 : 7, 8.)

39.

THE WEARING OF LONG HAIR BY MEN SANCTIONED.

And *no razor* shall come on his *head;* for the child shall be a Nazarite unto God from the womb. (Judg. 13 : 5.)

All the days of the vow of his separation there shall *no razor* come upon his *head;* until the days be fulfilled in the which he separateth himself unto the Lord, he shall be holy, and shall let the *locks of the hair* of his head *grow.* (Num. 6 : 5.)

THE WEARING OF LONG HAIR BY MEN **CONDEMNED.**

Doth not even nature itself teach you, that if a man have *long hair,* it is a *shame* unto him? (1 Cor. 11 : 14.)

40.

CIRCUMCISION INSTITUTED.

This is my covenant which ye shall keep between me and you and thy seed after thee: Every man and child among you shall be *circumcised.* (Gen. 17 : 10.)

CIRCUMCISION **CONDEMNED.**

Behold, I Paul, say unto you, that if ye be circumcised, *Christ shall profit you nothing.* (Gal. 5 : 2.)

41.

THE SABBATH INSTITUTED.

Remember the *Sabbath day* to keep it *holy.* (Ex. 20 : 8.)

THE SABBATH **REPUDIATED.**

The new moons and *sabbaths,* the calling of assemblies, I cannot away with; it is *iniquity.* (Is. 1 : 13.)

One man esteemeth one day above another; another esteemeth *every day alike.* Let every man be fully persuaded in his own mind. (Rom. 14 : 5.)

Let no man therefore judge you in meat and drink, or in respect of a *holy day,* or of the new moon; or of the *sabbath days.* (Col. 2 : 16.)

42.

THE SABBATH INSTITUTED BECAUSE GOD RESTED ON THE SEVENTH DAY.

For in six days the Lord made heaven and earth, the sea, and all that in them is, and *rested on the seventh day; wherefore* the Lord *blessed* the Sabbath day and *hallowed* it. (Ex. 20 : 11.)

THE SABBATH INSTITUTED **BECAUSE GOD BROUGHT THE ISRAELITES OUT OF EGYPT.**

And remember that thou wast a servant in the land of Egypt, and that the Lord thy God *brought thee out thence* through a mighty hand and a stretched out arm; *therefore* the Lord thy God commanded thee to *keep the Sabbath day.* (Deut. 5 : 15.)

43.

NO WORK TO BE DONE ON THE SABBATH UNDER PENALTY OF DEATH.

Whosoever doeth *any work* on the Sabbath day, he shall surely be *put to death.* (Ex. 31 : 15.)

And they found a man that *gathered sticks* upon the Sabbath day. . . . And all the congregation brought him without the camp and *stoned* him with stones, and *he died;* as the *Lord commanded Moses.* (Num. 15 : 32, 36.)

JESUS CHRIST **BROKE** THE SABBATH AND **JUSTIFIED HIS DISCIPLES** IN THE SAME.

Therefore did the Jews persecute Jesus, and sought to slay him, because he had *done these things* on the *Sabbath day.* (John 5 : 16.)

At that time Jesus went on the *Sabbath day* through the corn; and his disciples were a hungered, and began to pluck the ears of corn, and to eat. But when the Pharisees saw it they said unto him, Behold, thy disciples do that which is *not lawful* to do upon the Sabbath day. But he said unto them, ... Have ye not read in the law, how that on the Sabbath days the priests in the temple *profane* the Sabbath, and are *blameless?* (Matt. 12 : 1, 2, 3, 5.)

44.

BAPTISM COMMANDED.

Go ye therefore and teach all nations, *baptizing* them in the name of the Father, and of the Son, and of the Holy Ghost. (Matt. 28 : 19.)

BAPTISM **NOT** COMMANDED.

For Christ sent me *not to baptize,* but to preach the gospel. . . . I thank God that I *baptized none* of you but Crispus and Gaius. (1 Cor. 1 : 17, 14.)

45.

EVERY KIND OF ANIMAL ALLOWED FOR FOOD.

Every moving thing that liveth shall be meat for you. (Gen. 9 : 3.)

Whatsoever is sold in the shambles that *eat.* (1 Cor. 10 : 25.)

There is *nothing unclean* of itself. (Rom. 14 : 14.)

CERTAIN KINDS OF ANIMALS **PROHIBITED** FOR FOOD.

Nevertheless, these shall ye *not eat,* of them that chew the cud or of them that divide the cloven hoof; as the *camel* and the *hare,* and the *coney;* for they chew the cud, but but divide not the hoof; therefore, they are *unclean* unto you. And the *swine,* because it divideth the hoof, yet cheweth not the cud, it is unclean unto you; ye shall *not eat* of their flesh, nor touch their dead carcass. (Deut. 14 : 7, 8.)

46.

THE TAKING OF OATHS SANCTIONED.

If a man vow a vow unto the Lord, or swear an *oath* to bind his soul with a bond, he shall not break his word; he *shall do* according to all that proceedeth out of his mouth. (Num. 30 : 2.)

Now, therefore, *swear* unto me here by God. . . . And Abraham said, I will *swear.* . . . Therefore, he called the place Beersheba [the well of the oath]; because there they sware both of them. (Gen. 21 : 23, 24, 31.)

And Jacob *sware* by the fear of his father Isaac. (Gen. 31 : 53.)

Because he [God] could swear by no greater, he *sware* by himself. (Heb. 6 : 13.)

THE TAKING OF OATHS **FORBIDDEN.**

But I say unto you, *swear not at all;* neither by heaven for it is God's throne; nor by the earth for it is his footstool. (Matt. 5 : 34.)

47.

MARRIAGE APPROVED.

And the Lord God said, It is not good that the man should be alone: I will make a help-meet for him. (Gen. 2 : 18.)

And God said unto them, Be *fruitful* and *multiply,* and *replenish* the earth. (Gen. 1 : 28.)

For this cause shall a man leave father and mother and shall *cleave unto his wife.* (Matt. 19 : 5.)

Marriage is *honorable in all.* (Heb. 13 : 4.)

MARRIAGE **DISAPPROVED.**

It is good for a man *not to touch* a woman. (1 Cor. 7 : 1.)

For I [Paul] would that all men were even as *I myself.* . . . It is good for them if they abide even as *I.* (1 Cor. 7 : 7, 8.)

48.

FREEDOM OF DIVORCE PERMITTED.

When a man hath taken a wife and married her, and it come to pass that she found *no favor* in his eyes, . . . then let him write her a bill of *divorcement,* and give it in her hand, and send her *out of his house.* (Deut. 24 : 1.)

When thou goest out to war against thine enemies, and the Lord thy God hath delivered them into thy hands, and thou hast taken them captive, and seest among the captives a beautiful woman and hast a desire unto her, then thou shalt take her home to thy house; . . . and after that thou shalt *go in* unto her and be *her husband,* and she shall be *thy wife.* . . . And if thou have *no delight* in her, then thou shalt *let her go* whither she will; but thou shalt not sell her at all for money; thou shalt not make merchandise of her. (Deut. 21 : 10, 11, 14.)

DIVORCE **RESTRICTED.**

But I say unto you, that whosoever shall put away his wife, saving for the cause of *fornication,* causeth her to commit *adultery.* (Matt. 5 : 32.)

49.

ADULTERY FORBIDDEN.

Thou shalt not commit *adultery.* (Ex. 20 : 14.)
Whoremongers and *adulterers* God will judge. (Heb. 13 : 4.)

ADULTERY **ALLOWED.**

But all the *women children* that have not known a man by lying with him, keep *alive* for *yourselves.* (Num. 31 : 18.)
And the Lord said unto Hosea, Go, take thee a wife of whoredoms. . . . Then said the Lord to me [Hosea], Go, yet, *love a woman,* beloved of her friend, yet *an adulteress.* . . . So I *bought* her; . . . and said unto her, Thou shalt *abide for me* many days; thou shalt not play the harlot, and thou shalt not be for another man; so will I also be for thee. (Hos. 1 : 2, & 2 : 1, 2, 3.)

50.

MARRIAGE OR COHABITATION
WITH A SISTER DENOUNCED.

Cursed is he that lieth with his *sister,* the daughter of his father. (Deut. 27 : 22.)

And if a man shall take his *sister,* his father's daughter, or his mother's daughter, . . . it is a wicked thing. (Lev. 20 : 17.)

ABRAHAM MARRIED HIS SISTER
AND GOD **BLESSED THE UNION.**

And Abraham said, . . . She is my *sister;* she is the daughter of my *father,* but not the daughter of my mother. (Gen. 20 : 11, 12.)

And God said unto Abraham, as for Sarah thy wife, . . . I will *bless* her, and give thee a *son* also of her. (Gen. 17 : 16.)

51.

A MAN MAY MARRY HIS BROTHER'S WIDOW.

If brethren dwell together, and one of them die and have no child, the wife of the dead shall not marry without unto a stranger; her *husband's brother* shall come in unto her bed and take her to *wife.* (Deut. 25 : 5.)

A MAN MAY **NOT** MARRY HIS BROTHER'S WIDOW.

If a man shall take his *brother's wife,* it is an *unclean thing,* . . . they shall be childless. (Lev. 20 : 21.)

52.

HATRED TO KINDRED ENJOINED.

If any man come unto me, and *hate not* his *father,* and *mother,* and *wife,* and *children,* and *brother,* and *sisters,* yea, and his own life also, he cannot be my disciple. (Luke 14 : 26.)

HATRED TO KINDRED **CONDEMNED.**

Honor thy *father* and *mother.* (Eph. 6 : 2.)

Husbands love your *wives.* . . . For *no* man ever yet *hated* his *own flesh.* (Eph. 5 : 25, 29.)

Whosoever *hateth* his *brother* is a *murderer.* (1 John 3 : 15.)

53.

INTOXICATING BEVERAGES RECOMMENDED.

Give *strong drink* to him that is ready to perish, and *wine* to those that be of heavy hearts. Let him *drink* and forget his poverty, and remember his misery no more. (Prov. 31 : 6, 7.)

Drink no longer water, but use a *little wine* for thy stomach's sake, and thine often infirmities. (1 Tim. 5 : 23.)

Wine maketh glad the heart of man. (Ps. 104 : 15.)

INTOXICATING BEVERAGES **DISCOUNTENANCED.**

Wine is a *mocker,* strong drink is a *raging,* and whosoever is deceived thereby is not wise. (Prov. 20 : 1.)

Look not thou upon the wine when it is red; when it giveth his color in the cup. . . . At the last it *biteth* like a *serpent* and *stingeth* like an *adder.* (Prov. 23 : 31, 32.)

54.

IT IS OUR DUTY TO OBEY OUR RULERS, WHO ARE GOD'S MINISTERS AND PUNISH EVIL DOERS ONLY.

Let every soul be *subject* unto the *higher powers.* For there is *no power but of God;* the powers that be are *ordained of God.* Whosoever, therefore, *resisteth* the power, resisteth the *ordinance of God;* and they that resist shall receive to themselves *damnation.* For rulers are not a terror to *good works,* but to *evil.* . . . For this cause pay ye tribute; for they are *God's ministers,* attending continually upon this very thing. (Rom. 13 : 1, 2, 3, 6.)

The Scribes and Pharisees sit in Moses' seat; all, therefore, whatsoever they *bid* you observe, that *observe and do.* (Matt. 23 : 2, 3.)

Submit yourselves to *every ordinance of man* for the Lord's sake; whether it be to the king as supreme, or unto the governors as unto them that are *sent of him* for the *punishment of evil doers.* (1 Pet. 2 : 13, 14.)

I counsel thee to *keep the king's commandment.* . . . Whoso keepeth the commandment shall *feel no evil* thing. (Eccl. 8 : 2, 5.)

IT IS **NOT** OUR DUTY ALWAYS TO OBEY RULERS, WHO **SOMETIMES** PUNISH THE GOOD, AND RECEIVE UNTO THEMSELVES **DAMNATION** THEREFOR.

But the midwives feared God, and *did not* as the king of Egypt *commanded them.* . . . Therefore God dealt well with the midwives. (Ex. 1 : 17, 20.)

Shadrach, Meshach, and Abednego answered and said. . . . Be it known unto thee, O king, that we *will not serve thy gods, nor worship the golden image* which thou hast set up. (Dan. 3 : 16, 18.)

Therefore, king Darius signed the writing and the decree. . . . (that whosoever shall ask a *petition of any God* for

thirty days . . . he shall be cast into the den of lions). . . .
Now, when Daniel knew that the writing was signed, he
went into his house and . . . *kneeled* upon his knees three
times a day and *prayed* . . . as he did aforetime. (Dan. 6 : 9,
7, 10.)

And the *rulers* were gathered together *against the Lord*
and against his Christ. For of a truth, *against thy holy child
Jesus,* whom thou has anointed, both *Herod and Pontius
Pilate,* with the Gentiles, and the people of Israel, were
gathered together. (Acts 4 : 26, 27.)

Beware of the Scribes, which love to go in long clothing,
and love salutations in the market places, and the *chief
seats* in the synagogues. . . . These shall receive *greater
damnation.* (Mark 12 : 38, 39, 40.)

And *Herod* with his men of war *set him at naught,* and
mocked him, and arrayed him in a gorgeous robe, and sent
him again to Pilate. . . . And *Pilate gave sentence.* . . . And
when they were come to the place which is called Calvary,
there they *crucified him.* . . . And the people stood by behold-
ing. And the *rulers also* with them *derided* him. (Luke 23 :
11, 24, 33, 35.)

55.

WOMEN'S RIGHTS DENIED.

And thy desire shall be to thy husband, and he shall
rule over thee. (Gen. 3 : 16.)

I *suffer not a woman to teach,* nor to usurp authority
over the man, but to be *in silence.* (1 Tim. 2 : 12.)

They are commanded to be *under obedience,* as also
saith the law. (1 Cor. 14 : 34.)

Even as *Sarah obeyed Abraham,* calling him Lord.
(1 Pet. 3 : 6.)

WOMEN'S RIGHTS **AFFIRMED.**

And Deborah, a *prophetess, . . . judged Israel* at that time. . . . And Deborah said unto Barak, Up, for this is the day in which the Lord hath delivered Sisera into thy hand. . . . And the Lord discomfited Sisera, and all his chariots, and all his host, with the edge of the sword before Barak. (Judg. 4 : 4, 14, 15.)

The inhabitants of the villages ceased; they ceased in Israel, until I, *Deborah, arose,* a *mother in Israel.* (Judg. 5 : 7.)

And on my hand-maidens I will pour out in those days my spirit, and they *shall prophesy.* (Acts 2 : 18.)

And the same man had four daughters, virgins, which *did prophesy.* (Acts 21 : 9.)

56.

OBEDIENCE TO MASTERS ENJOINED.

Servants, *obey in all things your masters* after the flesh. . . . And whatsoever ye do, do it as heartily as to the Lord. (Col. 3 : 22, 23.)

Be *subject to your masters* with all fear; not only to the *good and gentle,* but also, to the *froward.* (1 Pet. 2 : 18.)

OBEDIENCE DUE TO GOD **ONLY.**

Thou shalt worship the Lord thy God, and *him only* shalt thou *serve.* (Matt. 4 : 10.)

Be not ye the servants of men. (1 Cor. 7 : 23.)

Neither be ye *called masters;* for *one* is your *master,* even *Christ.* (Matt. 23 : 10.)

57.

THERE IS AN UNPARDONABLE SIN.

He that shall blaspheme against the Holy Ghost hath *never forgiveness*. (Mark 3 : 29.)

THERE IS **NO** UNPARDONABLE SIN.

And by him *all* that *believe* are *justified* from *all things*. (Acts 13 : 39.)

HISTORICAL FACTS

58.

MAN WAS CREATED AFTER THE OTHER ANIMALS.

And God made the *beast* of the earth after his kind, and the *cattle* after their kind. . . . And God said, Let us make *man*. . . . So God *created man* in his own image. (Gen. 1: 25, 26, 27.)

MAN WAS CREATED **BEFORE** THE OTHER ANIMALS.

And the Lord God said it is not good that *man* should be *alone;* I will make a help-meet for him. And out of the ground the Lord God formed *every beast* of the field, and *every fowl* of the air, and *brought them unto Adam* to see what he would call them. (Gen. 2: 18, 19.)

59.

SEED TIME AND HARVEST WERE NEVER TO CEASE.

While the earth remaineth, *seed time* and *harvest* . . . shall *not cease*. (Gen. 8 : 22.)

SEED TIME AND HARVEST **DID CEASE** FOR SEVEN YEARS.

And the seven years of *dearth* began to come. . . . And the *famine* was over all the face of the earth. (Gen. 41 : 54, 56.)

For these two years hath *famine* been in the land; and yet there are *five years* in which there *shall neither be earing nor harvest.* (Gen. 45 : 6.)

60.

GOD HARDENED PHARAOH'S HEART.

But *I* will *harden* his *heart,* that he shall not let the people go. (Ex. 4: 21).
And the *Lord hardened* the *heart* of Pharaoh. (Ex. 9 : 12.)

PHARAOH HARDENED HIS **OWN** HEART.

But when Pharaoh saw that there was respite, *he hardened* his *heart,* and hearkened not unto them. (Ex. 8 : 15.)

61.

ALL THE CATTLE AND HORSES IN EGYPT DIED.

Behold, the hand of the Lord is upon thy cattle which is in the field, upon the *horses,* upon the asses, upon the camels, upon the oxen, and upon the sheep. . . . And *all the cattle of Egypt died.* (Ex. 9 : 3, 6.)

ALL THE HORSES OF EGYPT DID **NOT** DIE.

But the Egyptians pursued after them (all the *horses* and chariots of *Pharaoh,* and his *horsemen,* and his army) and overtook them encamping by the sea. (Ex. 14 : 9.)

62.

MOSES FEARED PHARAOH.

And Moses *feared,* and said, Surely this thing is known. Now, when Pharaoh heard this thing, he sought to slay Moses. But Moses fled before the face of Pharaoh, and dwelt in the land of Midian. . . . And it came to pass, in process of time, that the king of Egypt died. . . . And the Lord said unto Moses, in Midian, Go, return unto Egypt; for all the men are dead which sought thy life. (Ex. 2 : 14, 15, 23; & 4 : 19.)

MOSES DID **NOT** FEAR PHARAOH.

By faith he [Moses] forsook Egypt, *not fearing* the wrath of the king. (Heb. 11 : 27.)

63.

THERE DIED OF THE PLAGUE TWENTY-FOUR THOUSAND.

And those that died in the plague were *twenty and four thousand.* (Num. 25 : 9.)

THERE DIED OF THE PLAGUE BUT **TWENTY-THREE THOUSAND.**

And fell in one day *three and twenty thousand.* (1 Cor. 10 : 8.)

64.

JOHN THE BAPTIST WAS ELIAS.

This is *Elias* which was to come. (Matt. 11 : 14.)

JOHN THE BAPTIST WAS **NOT** ELIAS.

And they asked him, What then? Art thou *Elias?* and he said I am *not.* (John 1 : 21.)

65.

THE FATHER OF JOSEPH, MARY'S HUSBAND, WAS JACOB.

And *Jacob begat Joseph,* the husband of Mary, of whom was born Jesus. (Matt. 1 : 16.)

THE FATHER OF MARY'S HUSBAND WAS **HELI.**

Being the son of *Joseph* which was the *son of Heli.* (Luke 3 : 23.)

66.

THE FATHER OF SALAH WAS ARPHAXAD.

And Arphaxad lived *five and thirty years* and *begat Salah.* (Gen. 11 : 12.)

THE FATHER OF SALAH WAS **CAINAN.**

Which was the son of Sala, which was the son of *Cainan,* which was the son of Arphaxad. (Luke 3 : 35, 36.)

67.

THERE WERE FOURTEEN GENERATIONS FROM ABRAHAM TO DAVID.

So all the generations from *Abraham to David* are fourteen generations. (Matt. 1 : 17.)

THERE WERE BUT **THIRTEEN** GENERATIONS FROM ABRAHAM TO DAVID.

Abraham begat Isaac . . . Jacob . . . Judas . . . Phares . . . Esrom . . . Aram . . . Aminaldab . . . Naason . . . Salmon . . . Booz . . . Obed . . . Jesse . . . David . . . [13]. (Matt. 1 : 2, 3, 4, 5, 6.)

68.

THERE WERE FOURTEEN GENERATIONS FROM THE BABYLONISH CAPTIVITY TO CHRIST.

And from the carrying away into *Babylon unto Christ* are *fourteen generations.* (Matt. 1 : 17.)

THERE WERE BUT **THIRTEEN** GENERATIONS FROM THE BABYLONISH CAPTIVITY TO CHRIST.

And after they were brought to Babylon Jechonias begat Salathiel . . . Zorobabel . . . Abiud . . . Eliakim . . . Azor . . . Sadoc . . . Achim . . . Eliud . . . Eleazar . . . Matthan . . . Jacob . . . Joseph, the husband of Mary, of whom was born Jesus [13]. (Matt. 1 : 12, 13, 14, 15, 16.)

69.

THE INFANT CHRIST WAS TAKEN INTO EGYPT.

When he arose he took the young child and his mother by night and departed into Egypt, and was there until the death of Herod. . . . But when Herod was dead, . . . he took the young child and his mother and came . . . and dwelt in a city called Nazareth. (Matt. 2 : 14, 15, 19, 21, 23.)

THE INFANT CHRIST WAS **NOT** TAKEN INTO EGYPT.

And when the days of her purification, according to the law of Moses, were accomplished, they brought him to Jerusalem, to present him to the Lord. . . . And when they had performed all things, according to the law of the Lord they returned . . . to their own city, Nazareth. (Luke 2 : 22, 39.)

70.

CHRIST WAS TEMPTED IN THE WILDERNESS.

And *immediately* [after Christ's baptism] the spirit driveth him *into the wilderness*. And he was there in the wilderness *forty days* tempted of Satan. (Mark 1 : 12, 13.)

CHRIST WAS **NOT** TEMPTED IN THE WILDERNESS.

And the *third day* [after Christ's baptism] there was a marriage in Cana of Galilee. . . . Both *Jesus was called* and his disciples *to the marriage*. (John 2 : 1, 2.)

71.

CHRIST PREACHED HIS FIRST SERMON ON THE MOUNT.

And seeing the multitude he went up into a *mountain,* and when he was *set* his *disciples came unto him*. And he *opened* his *mouth* and *taught* them, saying. (Matt. 5 : 1, 2.)

CHRIST PREACHED HIS FIRST SERMON IN THE **PLAIN.**

And he *came down with them and stood in the plain;* and the company of his disciples, and a great multitude of people . . . came to hear him. . . . And he lifted up his eyes on his disciples and said. (Luke 6 : 17, 20.)

72.

JOHN WAS IN PRISON WHEN
JESUS WENT INTO GALILEE.

Now, *after that John was put in prison Jesus came into Galilee* preaching the gospel of the kingdom of God. (Mark 1 : 14.)

JOHN WAS **NOT** IN PRISON WHEN
JESUS WENT INTO GALILEE.

The day following Jesus would go forth *into Galilee.* (John 1 : 43.)

And after these things came Jesus with his disciples into the land of Judea. . . . And *John was baptizing* in Enon. . . . For *John was* NOT YET *cast into prison.* (John 3 : 22, 23, 24.)

73.

CHRIST'S DISCIPLES WERE COMMANDED TO GO FORTH
WITH A STAFF AND SANDALS.

And commanded them that they should take nothing for their journey, save a *staff only;* no scrip, no bread, no money in their purse; but be shod with *sandals.* (Mark 6 : 8, 9.)

CHRIST'S DISCIPLES WERE COMMANDED TO GO FORTH
WITH **NEITHER** STAVES NOR SANDALS.

Provide neither gold, nor silver, nor brass in your purses; nor scrip for your journey, neither two coats, *neither shoes, nor yet staves.* (Matt. 10 : 9, 10.)

74.

A WOMAN OF CANAAN BESOUGHT JESUS.

And behold, a woman of *Canaan* came out of the same coasts, and cried unto him, Have mercy on me, O Lord, thou son of David; my daughter is grievously vexed with a devil. (Matt. 15 : 22.)

IT WAS A **GREEK** WOMAN WHO BESOUGHT HIM.

The woman was a *Greek,* a *Syrophenician* by nation, and she besought him that he would cast forth the devil out of her daughter. (Mark 7 : 26.)

75.

TWO BLIND MEN BESOUGHT JESUS.

And behold, *two blind men* sitting by the way-side, when they heard that Jesus passed by, cried out, saying, Have mercy on us, O Lord thou son of David. (Matt. 20 : 30.)

ONLY **ONE** BLIND MAN BESOUGHT HIM.

A certain *blind man* sat by the way-side begging. . . . And he cried, saying, Jesus, thou son of David, have mercy on me. (Luke 18 : 35, 38.)

76.

CHRIST WAS CRUCIFIED AT THE THIRD HOUR.

And it was the *third hour* and they crucified him. (Mark 15 : 25.)

CHRIST WAS NOT CRUCIFIED UNTIL THE **SIXTH** HOUR.

And it was the preparation of the passover, and about the *sixth hour;* and he saith unto the Jews, Behold your king. . . . *Shall I crucify* your king? (John 19 : 14, 15.)

77.

THE TWO THIEVES REVILED CHRIST.

The thieves also, which were crucified with him, cast the same in his teeth. (Matt. 27 : 44.)
And *they that were crucified* reviled him. (Mark 15 : 32.)

ONLY **ONE** OF THE THIEVES REVILED CHRIST.

And *one* of the malefactors which were hanged railed on him. . . . But the *other* answering *rebuked him,* saying, Dost thou not fear God, seeing thou art in the same condemnation? (Luke 23 : 39, 40.)

78.

SATAN ENTERED INTO JUDAS WHILE AT THE SUPPER.

And after the sop *Satan entered* into him. (John 13 : 27.)

SATAN ENTERED INTO HIM **BEFORE** THE SUPPER.

Then entered Satan into Judas, . . . and he went his way and communed with the chief priests and captains, how he might betray him. . . . *Then* came the day of unleavened bread when the *passover* must be killed. (Luke 22 : 3, 4, 7.)

79.

JUDAS COMMITTED SUICIDE BY HANGING.

And he cast down the pieces of silver into the temple, and departed, and went out and *hanged* himself. (Matt. 27 : 5.)

JUDAS DID **NOT** HANG HIMSELF, BUT DIED ANOTHER WAY.

And falling headlong he *burst asunder* in the midst, and all his *bowels gushed out.* (Acts 1 : 18.)

80.

THE POTTER'S FIELD WAS PURCHASED BY JUDAS.

Now, *this man purchased a field* with the reward of iniquity. (Acts 1 : 18.)

THE POTTER'S FIELD WAS PURCHASED BY THE **CHIEF PRIESTS.**

And the *chief priests took the silver pieces, . . . and bought* with them the *potter's field.* (Matt. 27 : 6, 7.)

81.

THERE WAS BUT ONE WOMAN WHO CAME TO THE SEPULCHRE.

The first day of the week cometh *Mary Magdalene*, early, when it was yet dark, unto the sepulchre. (John 20 : 1.)

THERE WERE **TWO** WOMEN WHO CAME
TO THE SEPULCHRE.

In the end of the Sabbath, as it began to dawn towards the first day of the week, came *Mary Magdalene, and the* OTHER MARY to the sepulchre. (Matt. 28 : 1.)

82.

THERE WERE THREE WOMEN WHO CAME
TO THE SEPULCHRE.

When the Sabbath was past, *Mary Magdalene,* and *Mary the mother of James,* and *Salome,* had brought sweet spices, that that they might come and anoint him. (Mark 16 : 1.)

THERE WERE **MORE THAN THREE** WOMEN
WHO CAME TO THE SEPULCHRE.

It was *Mary Magdalene and Mary the mother of James, and* OTHER WOMEN that were with them. (Luke 24 : 10.)

83.

IT WAS AT SUNRISE WHEN THEY CAME
TO THE SEPULCHRE.

And very early in the morning, the first day of the week, they came unto the sepulchre, at the *rising of the sun.* (Mark: 16 : 2.)

IT WAS **SOME TIME BEFORE** SUNRISE
WHEN THEY CAME.

The first day of the week, cometh Mary Magdalene, early, *while it was yet dark,* unto the sepulchre. (John 20 : 1.)

84.

THERE WERE TWO ANGELS SEEN BY THE WOMEN AT THE SEPULCHRE, AND THEY WERE STANDING UP.

And it came to pass, as they were much perplexed thereabout, behold, *two men stood* by him in *shining garments.* (Luke 24 : 4.)

THERE WAS BUT **ONE** ANGEL SEEN, AND HE WAS **SITTING DOWN.**

For *the angel* of the Lord descended from heaven, and came and rolled back the stone from the door, and *sat* upon it. . . . And *the angel* answered and said unto the women, Fear not. (Matt. 28 : 2, 5.)

85.

THERE WERE TWO ANGELS SEEN WITHIN THE SEPULCHRE.

And as she wept she stooped down and looked into the sepulchre, and seeth *two angels in white.* (John 20 : 11, 12.)

THERE WAS BUT **ONE** ANGEL SEEN WITHIN THE SEPULCHRE.

And entering into the sepulchre, they saw *a young man* sitting on the right side, clothed in a *long white garment.* (Mark 16 : 5.)

86.

CHRIST WAS TO BE THREE DAYS AND THREE NIGHTS IN THE GRAVE.

So shall the son of man be *three days and three nights* in the heart of the earth. (Matt. 12 : 40.)

CHRIST WAS BUT **TWO** DAYS AND **TWO** NIGHTS IN THE GRAVE.

And it was the *third hour,* and they crucified him. . . . It was the preparation, that is, the *day before the Sabbath.* . . . And Pilate . . . gave the body to Joseph. And he . . . laid him in a sepulchre. . . . Now, when Jesus was risen *early* the *first day of the week,* he appeared first to Mary Magdalene. (Mark 15 : 25, 42, 44, 45, 46; & 16 : 9.)

87.

THE HOLY GHOST BESTOWED AT PENTECOST.

But ye shall receive power after that the Holy Ghost is come upon you. . . . Ye shall be baptized with the Holy Ghost *not many days hence.* (Acts 1 : 8, 5.)

And when the day of Pentecost was fully come they were all of one accord in one place. . . . And they were *all filled with the Holy Ghost.* (Acts 2 : 1, 4.)

THE HOLY GHOST BESTOWED **BEFORE** PENTECOST.

And when he had said this he breathed on them, and said unto them, *Receive ye the Holy Ghost.* (John 20 : 22.)

88.

THE DISCIPLES WERE COMMANDED IMMEDIATELY AFTER THE RESURRECTION TO GO INTO GALILEE.

Then said Jesus unto them, Be not afraid; go tell my brethren that they *go into Galilee,* and there shall they see me. (Matt. 28 : 10.)

THE DISCIPLES WERE COMMANDED IMMEDIATELY AFTER THE RESURRECTION TO **TARRY AT JERUSALEM.**

But *tarry ye in Jerusalem* until ye be endued with power from on high. (Luke 24 : 49.)

89.

JESUS FIRST APPEARED TO THE ELEVEN DISCIPLES IN A ROOM AT JERUSALEM.

And they rose up the same hour and returned to *Jerusalem,* and found the eleven gathered together. . . . And as they spake, Jesus himself *stood up in the midst of* them. . . . But they were terrified and affrighted, and supposed that they had seen a *spirit.* (Luke 24 : 33, 36, 37.)

The same day, at evening, being the first day of the week, when the *doors* were *shut,* where the *disciples* were *assembled,* . . . came Jesus and *stood in the midst.* (John 20 : 19.)

JESUS FIRST APPEARED TO THE ELEVEN ON A **MOUNTAIN** IN **GALILEE.**

Then the eleven disciples went away into *Galilee,* unto a *mountain* where Jesus had appointed. And when they saw him they worshipped him, but some *doubted.* (Matt. 28 : 16, 17.)

90.

CHRIST ASCENDED FROM MOUNT OLIVET.

And when he had spoken these things, while they beheld, he was taken up, and a cloud received him out of their sight. . . . Then returned they unto Jerusalem, *from the mount called Olivet.* (Acts 1 : 9, 12.)

CHRIST ASCENDED FROM **BETHANY.**

And he led them out as far as to *Bethany;* and he lifted up his hands and blessed them. And it came to pass that while he blessed them, he was parted from them, and *carried up into heaven.* (Luke 24 : 50, 51.)

91.

PAUL'S ATTENDANTS HEARD THE MIRACULOUS VOICE, AND STOOD SPEECHLESS.

And the men which journeyed with him [Paul] *stood speechless, hearing* a voice but seeing no man. (Acts 9 : 7.)

PAUL'S ATTENDANTS HEARD **NOT** THE VOICE, AND WERE PROSTRATE.

And they that were with me saw indeed the light and were afraid; but they *heard not the voice* of him that spake to me. (Acts 22 : 9.)

And when we were *all fallen to the earth,* I heard a voice. (Acts 26 : 14.)

92.

ABRAHAM DEPARTED TO GO INTO CANAAN.

And Abram took Sarah his wife, and Lot, his brother's son, . . . and they went forth *to go* into the land of *Canaan, and into the land of Canaan* they *came.* (Gen. 12 : 5.)

ABRAHAM WENT NOT KNOWING **WHERE.**

By faith Abraham when he was called to go out into a place which he should after receive for an inheritance, obeyed; and he went out *not knowing whither he went.* (Heb. 11 : 8.)

93.

ABRAHAM HAD TWO SONS.

Abraham had *two sons;* the one by a bond-woman, and the other by a free woman. (Gal. 4 : 22.)

ABRAHAM HAD BUT **ONE** SON.

By faith Abraham when he was tried, offered up Isaac, . . . his *only begotten son.* (Heb. 11 : 17.)

94.

KETURAH WAS ABRAHAM'S WIFE.

Then again Abraham took a *wife,* and her name was Keturah. (Gen. 25 : 1.)

KETURAH WAS ABRAHAM'S **CONCUBINE.**

The sons of Keturah, Abraham's *concubine.* (1 Chron. 1 : 32.)

95.

ABRAHAM BEGAT A SON WHEN HE WAS A HUNDRED YEARS OLD, BY THE INTERPOSITION OF PROVIDENCE.

Sarah conceived and bare Abraham a son in his *old age,* at the set time of which God had spoken to him. (Gen. 21 : 2.)

And being not weak in the *faith,* he considered not his own body, *now dead,* when he was a *hundred years old.* (Rom. 4: 19.)

Therefore sprang there even from one, and him *as good as dead,* so many as the stars of the sky. (Heb. 11 : 12.)

ABRAHAM BEGAT SIX CHILDREN MORE AFTER HE WAS A HUNDRED YEARS OLD, WITHOUT ANY INTERPOSITION OF PROVIDENCE.

Then *again* Abraham took a wife and her name was Keturah; and she bare him *Zimram,* and *Jockshan,* and *Medan,* and *Midian,* and *Ishbak,* and *Shuah.* (Gen. 25 : 1, 2.)

96.

JACOB BOUGHT A SEPULCHRE FROM HAMOR.

And the bones of Joseph . . . buried they in Shechem, in a parcel of ground which *Jacob* bought of the sons of *Hamor,* the father of Shechem. (Josh. 24 : 32.)

ABRAHAM BOUGHT IT OF HAMOR.

In the sepulchre that *Abraham* bought for a sum of money of the sons of *Emor,* the father of Sychem. (Acts 7 : 16.)

97.

GOD PROMISED THE LAND OF CANAAN
TO ABRAHAM AND HIS SEED FOREVER.

And the Lord said unto Abraham, after Lot was separated from him, Lift up now thine eyes and look from the place where thou art, northward and southward, and eastward and westward; for *all the land* which thou *seest,* to *thee* will I *give* it and to *thy seed forever.* . . . For I will give it unto thee. . . . Unto thee and to *thy seed after thee.* (Gen. 13 : 14, 15, 17; & 17 : 8.)

ABRAHAM AND HIS SEED **NEVER RECEIVED**
THE PROMISED LAND.

And he gave him [Abraham] *none inheritance* in it, no, not so much as to set his *foot* on. (Acts 7 : 5.)

By faith he *sojourned* in the land of promise as in a *strange country,* dwelling in tents with *Isaac* and *Jacob,* the heirs with him of the same promise. . . . These all died in faith, *not having received the promises.* (Heb. 11 : 9, 13.)

98.

GOLIATH WAS SLAIN BY ELHANAN.

And there was again a battle in Gob with the Philistines, where *Elhanan* the son of Jaare-oregim a Bethlehemite, slew ["the brother of," supplied by the translators] *Goliath* the Gittite, the staff of whose spear was like a weaver's beam. (2 Sam. 21 : 19.)

THE **BROTHER** OF GOLIATH WAS SLAIN BY ELHANAN.

And there was war again with the Philistines, and *Elhanan* the son of Jair slew Lahmi *the brother of Goliath* the

Gittite, whose spear's staff was like a weaver's beam. (1 Chron. 20 : 5.)

99.

AHAZIAH BEGAN TO REIGN
IN THE TWELFTH YEAR OF JORAM.

In the *twelfth* year of Joram, the son of Ahab, king of Israel, did Ahaziah the son of Jehoram king of Judah begin to reign. (2 Kings 8 : 25.)

AHAZIAH BEGAN TO REIGN
IN THE **ELEVENTH** YEAR OF JORAM.

In the *eleventh* year of Joram the son of Ahab began Ahaziah to reign over Judah. (2 Kings 9 : 29.)

100.

MICHAL HAD NO CHILD.

Therefore Michal the daughter of Saul, had *no child* unto the day of her death. (2 Sam. 6 : 23.)

MICHAL HAD **FIVE** CHILDREN.

The *five sons of Michal* the daughter of Saul. (2 Sam. 21 : 8.)

101.

DAVID WAS TEMPTED BY THE LORD
TO NUMBER ISRAEL.

And the anger of the Lord was kindled against Israel,

and he moved David against them to say, Go number Israel and Judah. (2 Sam. 24 : 1.)

DAVID WAS TEMPTED BY **SATAN**
TO NUMBER THE PEOPLE.

And *Satan* stood up against Israel and provoked David to number Israel. (1 Chron. 21 : 1.)

102.

THE NUMBER OF FIGHTING MEN OF ISRAEL
WAS 800,000; AND OF JUDAH 500,000.

And Joab gave up the sum of the number of the people unto the king; and there were in Israel *eight hundred thousand* valiant men that drew the sword; and the men of Judah *five hundred thousand* men. (2 Sam. 24 : 9.)

THE NUMBER OF FIGHTING MEN OF ISRAEL WAS
1,100,000; AND OF JUDAH **470,000.**

And Joab gave the sum of the number of the people unto David. And all they of Israel were a *thousand thousand and a hundred thousand* [1,100,000] men that drew sword; and Judah was *four hundred three score and ten thousand* [470,000] men that drew sword. (1 Chron. 21 : 5.)

103.

DAVID SINNED IN NUMBERING THE PEOPLE.

And David's heart smote him after that he had numbered the people. And David said unto the Lord, *I have sinned* greatly in that I have done. (2 Sam. 24 : 10.)

DAVID **NEVER** SINNED,
EXCEPT IN THE MATTER OF URIAH.

David did that which was *right* in the eyes of the Lord, and *turned not aside from anything that he commanded him all the days of his life, save only in the matter of Uriah the Hittite.* (1 Kings 15 : 5.)

104.

ONE OF THE PENALTIES OF DAVID'S SIN
WAS SEVEN YEARS OF FAMINE.

So Gad came to David and told him, Shall *seven years of famine* come unto thee in thy land? (2 Sam. 24 : 13.)

IT WAS NOT SEVEN YEARS,
BUT **THREE** YEARS OF FAMINE.

So Gad came to David and said unto him, Thus saith the Lord, choose thee either *three* years of famine. (1 Chron. 21 : 11, 12.)

105.

DAVID TOOK SEVEN HUNDRED HORSEMEN.

And David took from him a thousand chariots and *seven hundred* horsemen. (2 Sam. 8 : 4.)

DAVID TOOK **SEVEN THOUSAND** HORSEMEN.

And David took from him a thousand chariots and *seven thousand* horsemen. (1 Chron. 18 : 4.)

106.

DAVID BOUGHT A THRESHING FLOOR
FOR FIFTY SHEKELS OF SILVER.

So David bought the threshing floor and the oxen for *fifty shekels of silver.* (2 Sam. 24 : 24.)

DAVID BOUGHT THE THRESHING FLOOR
FOR **SIX HUNDRED** SHEKELS OF GOLD.

So David gave to Ornan for the place *six hundred shekels of gold.* (1 Chron. 21 : 25.)

107.

DAVID'S THRONE WAS TO ENDURE FOREVER.

Once have I sworn by my holiness that I will not lie unto David. His seed shall endure forever and his *throne* as the *sun* before me. It shall be *established forever.* (Ps. 89 : 35, 36, 37.)

DAVID'S THRONE WAS **CAST DOWN.**

Thou hast made his glory to cease and hast *cast his throne down to the ground.* (Ps. 89 : 44.)

SPECULATIVE
DOCTRINES

108.

CHRIST IS EQUAL WITH GOD.

I and my Father are *one*. (John 10 : 30.)
Who, being in the form of God, thought it not robbery to be *equal with God*. (Phil. 2 : 5.)

CHRIST IS **NOT** EQUAL WITH GOD.

My father is *greater* than I. (John 14 : 28.)
Of that day and hour knoweth no man, not the angels of heaven, but my *Father only*. (Matt. 24 : 36.)

109.

JESUS WAS ALL-POWERFUL

All power is given unto me in heaven and in earth. (Matt. 28 : 18.)
The Father loveth the Son and hath given *all things into his hand*. (John 3 : 35.)

JESUS WAS **NOT** ALL-POWERFUL.

And *he could there do no mighty work,* save that he laid his hands on a few sick folk and healed them. (Mark 6 : 5.)

110.

THE LAW WAS SUPERSEDED
BY THE CHRISTIAN DISPENSATION.

The law and the prophets were *until* John; since that time the *kingdom of God* is preached. (Luke 16 : 16.)

Having *abolished* in the flesh the enmity, even the *law of commandments* contained in *ordinances*. (Eph. 2 : 15.)

But now we are *delivered from the law*. (Rom. 7 : 6.)

THE LAW WAS **NOT** SUPERSEDED
BY THE CHRISTIAN DISPENSATION.

I am come *not to destroy the law* but to fulfill. For verily I say unto you, till heaven and earth pass, one *jot* or one *tittle* shall *in no wise pass from the law* till all be fulfilled. Whosoever therefore shall break one of the *least commandments* and shall teach men so, he shall be called the least in the kingdom of heaven. (Matt. 5 : 17, 18, 19.)

111.

CHRIST'S MISSION WAS PEACE.

And suddenly there was with the angels a multitude of the heavenly host praising God and saying, Glory to God in the highest, and *on earth peace*. (Luke 2 : 13, 14.)

CHRIST'S MISSION WAS **NOT** PEACE.

Think not that I am come to send *peace on earth;* I *came not to send peace,* but a sword. (Matt. 10 : 34.)

112.

CHRIST RECEIVED NOT TESTIMONY FROM MAN.

Ye sent unto John and he bare witness unto the truth. But I receive *not testimony from man.* (John 5 : 33, 34.)

CHRIST **DID** RECEIVE TESTIMONY FROM MAN.

And ye shall also *bear witness,* because ye have been *with me* from the beginning. (John 15 : 27.)

113.

CHRIST'S WITNESS OF HIMSELF IS TRUE.

I am one that bear witness of myself. . . . Though I bear record of myself, yet *my record is true.* (John 8 : 18, 14.)

CHRIST'S WITNESS OF HIMSELF IS **NOT** TRUE.

If I bear witness of myself, *my witness is not true.* (John 5 : 31.)

114.

CHRIST LAID DOWN HIS LIFE FOR HIS FRIENDS.

Greater love hath no man than this, that a man *lay down his life for his friends.* (John 15 : 13.)

The good *shepherd* giveth his life for the *sheep.* (John 10 : 11.)

CHRIST LAID DOWN HIS LIFE FOR HIS **ENEMIES.**

When we were *enemies,* we were reconciled to God by the *death* of his Son. (Rom. 5 : 10.)

115.

IT WAS LAWFUL FOR THE JEWS
TO PUT CHRIST TO DEATH.

The Jews answered him, We have a *law,* and by our law he *ought to die.* (John 19 : 7.)

IT WAS **NOT** LAWFUL FOR THE JEWS
TO PUT HIM TO DEATH.

The Jews therefore said unto him, It is *not lawful* for us to put *any man to death.* (John 18 : 31.)

116.

CHILDREN ARE PUNISHED FOR THE SINS
OF THEIR PARENTS.

I am a jealous God, *visiting the iniquities of the fathers upon the children.* (Ex. 20 : 5.)

CHILDREN ARE **NOT** PUNISHED
FOR THE SINS OF THEIR PARENTS.

The *son* shall *not* bear the iniquities of the *father.* (Ezek. 18 : 20.)

117.

MAN IS JUSTIFIED BY FAITH ALONE.

By the deeds of the *law* there shall *no flesh be justified.* (Rom. 3 : 20.)

Knowing that a man is *not justified by the works of the law,* but by the faith of Jesus Christ. (Gal. 2 : 16.)

The *just* shall live by faith. And the *law* is *not* of faith. (Gal. 3: 11, 12.)

For *if* Abraham were justified by *works* he hath whereof to glory. (Rom. 4 : 2.)

MAN IS **NOT** JUSTIFIED BY FAITH ALONE.

Was not Abraham our father *justified by works?* . . . Ye see then how that *by works a man is justified, and not by faith only.* (James 2 : 21, 24.)

The *doers* of the *law* shall be justified. (Rom. 2 : 13.)

118.

IT IS IMPOSSIBLE TO FALL FROM GRACE.

And I give unto them eternal life, and they shall *never perish,* neither shall any pluck them out of my hand. (John 10 : 28.)

Neither death, nor life, nor angels, nor principalities, nor powers, nor things present, nor things to come, nor height nor depth, nor any other creature, shall *be able to separate us* from the love of God which is in Christ our Lord. (Rom. 8 : 38, 39.)

IT **IS** POSSIBLE TO FALL FROM GRACE.

But when the *righteous* man *turneth away* from his righteousness, and *committeth iniquity,* and doeth according to all the abominations that the wicked man doeth, shall he *live?* All his righteousness that he hath done shall not be mentioned; in his *trespass* that he hath trespassed, and in his *sin* that he hath sinned, in them shall he *die.* (Ezek. 18 : 24.)

For it is possible for those who were *once enlightened,* and have *tasted* of the *heavenly gift,* and are made *par-*

takers of the *Holy Ghost,* and have *tasted* the good *word of God,* and the *powers of the world to come,* if they *shall fall away,* to *renew* them *again* unto repentance. (Heb. 6 : 4, 5, 6.)

For if, after they have escaped the pollutions of the world through the knowledge of the Lord and Saviour Jesus Christ, they are *again entangled therein and overcome,* the latter end is worse than the beginning. For it had been better for them *not to have known* the way of righteousness, than after they had known it, to *turn from the holy commandment* delivered unto them. (2 Pet. 2 : 20, 21.)

119.

NO MAN IS WITHOUT SIN.

For there is *no* man that *sinneth not.* (1 Kings 8 : 46.)

Who can say, I have made my heart *clean;* I am *pure* from my *sin?* (Prov. 20 : 9.)

For there is *not a just man* upon earth, that doeth good and *sinneth not.* (Eccl. 7 : 20.)

There is *none* righteous, no, not *one.* (Rom. 3 : 10.)

CHRISTIANS ARE **SINLESS.**

Whosoever is born of God *doth not commit sin;* . . . he *cannot sin,* because he is born of God. . . . Whosoever abideth in him *sinneth not.* He that committeth sin is of the devil. (1 John 3 : 9, 6, 8.)

120.

THERE IS TO BE A RESURRECTION OF THE DEAD.

The trumpet shall sound and the *dead* shall be *raised.* (1 Cor. 15 : 52.)

And I saw the *dead,* small and great, *stand* before God; . . . and they were judged, every man according to their works. (Rev. 20 : 12, 13.)

Now that the *dead are raised* even Moses showed at the bush, when he called the Lord the God of Abraham, and the God of Isaac, and the God of Jacob. (Luke 20 : 37.)

For if the dead *rise* not, then is not Christ raised. (1 Cor. 15 : 16.)

THERE IS TO BE **NO** RESURRECTION OF THE DEAD.

As the cloud is consumed and vanisheth away, so he that goeth down to the *grave* shall *come up no more.* (Job 7 : 9.)

The dead *know not anything,* neither have they any more a *reward.* (Eccl. 9 : 5.)

They are dead, they *shall not live;* they are deceased they *shall not rise.* (Is. 26 : 14.)

121.

REWARD AND PUNISHMENT TO BE
BESTOWED IN THIS WORLD.

Behold the righteous shall be *recompensed* in the earth, much more the *wicked* and the *sinner.* (Prov. 11 : 31.)

REWARD AND PUNISHMENT TO BE
BESTOWED IN THE **NEXT** WORLD.

And the *dead were judged* out of those things which were written in the books, *according* to their *works.* (Rev. 20 : 12.)

Then he shall *reward* every man according to his *works.* (Matt. 16 : 27.)

According to that he hath *done,* whether it be *good* or *bad.* (2 Cor. 5 : 10.)

122.

ANNIHILATION THE PORTION OF ALL MANKIND.

Why died I not from the womb? Why did I not give up the ghost when I came out of the belly? . . . For now should I have *lain still* and *been quiet;* I should have *slept;* then had I been at *rest,* with kings and counsellors of the earth, which built desolate places for themselves; or with princes that had gold, who filled their houses with silver; or as a *hidden, untimely birth* I had not been; as *infants* which *never saw light.* THERE the wicked *cease from troubling,* and there the weary be *at rest.* . . . The small and great are there, and the servant is free from his master. Wherefore is light given to him that is in misery, and *life* unto the bitter in soul, which long for *death* and it cometh not, . . . which rejoice exceedingly when they have found the *grave?* (Job 3 : 11, 13-17, 19, 20, 21, 22.)

The dead know not anything. . . . For there is no work, nor device, nor *knowledge,* nor *wisdom* in the grave whither thou goest. (Eccl. 9 : 5, 10.)

For that which befalleth the sons of *men* befalleth the *beasts,* even *one thing* befalleth them; as the *one* dieth, so dieth the *other;* yea, they have *all one breath;* so that a man hath no preeminence above a beast. . . . All go unto *one place.* (Eccl. 3 : 19, 20.)

ENDLESS MISERY THE PORTION OF A PART OF MANKIND.

These shall go away unto *everlasting punishment.* (Matt. 25 : 46.)

And the devil that deceived them was cast into the lake of fire and brimstone, where the beast and the false prophet are, and shall be *tormented day and night for ever and ever.* . . . And whosoever was not found written in the book of life was cast into the lake of fire. (Rev. 20 : 10, 15.)

And the smoke of their *torment* ascendeth up *forever and ever.* (Rev. 14 : 11.)

And many of them that sleep in the dust shall awake, some to everlasting life, and some to shame and *everlasting contempt.* (Dan. 12 : 2.)

123.

THE EARTH IS TO BE DESTROYED.

The earth also and the works that are therein shall be *burned up.* (2 Pet. 3 : 10.)

They shall perish, but thou remainest. (Heb. 1 : 11.)

And I saw a great white throne, and him that sat on it, from whose face the *earth* and the heaven *fled away,* and there was *no place* found for them. (Rev. 20 : 11.)

THE EARTH IS **NEVER** TO BE DESTROYED.

Who laid the foundations of the *earth* that it *should not be removed forever.* (Ps. 104 : 5.)

But the *earth abideth forever.* (Eccl. 1 : 4.)

124.

NO EVIL SHALL HAPPEN TO THE GODLY.

There shall *no evil* happen to the *just.* (Prov. 12 : 21.)

Who is he that will *harm* you, if ye be followers of that which is *good?* (1 Pet. 3 : 13.)

EVIL **DOES** HAPPEN TO THE GODLY.

Whom the Lord loveth he *chasteneth,* and *scourgeth* every *son* whom he receiveth. (Heb. 12 : 6.)

And the Lord said unto Satan, Hast thou considered my servant Job, that there is none like him, a *perfect* and an *upright* man? . . . So went Satan forth . . . and *smote* Job with *sore boils* from the sole of his foot unto the crown of his head. (Job 2 : 3, 7.)

125.

WORLDLY GOOD AND PROSPERITY ARE THE LOT OF THE GODLY.

There shall *no evil* happen to the *just.* (Prov. 12 : 21.)

For the Lord loveth judgment and forsaketh not his *saints;* they are *preserved forever.* . . . The wicked watcheth for the righteous and seeketh to slay him. The Lord *will not leave him* in his hand, nor condemn him when he is judged. . . . Mark the perfect man, and behold the upright; for the *end* of that man is *peace.* (Ps. 37 : 28, 32, 33, 37.)

Blessed is the man that walketh not in the counsel of the ungodly. . . . *Whatsoever he doeth shall prosper.* (Ps. 1 : 1, 3.)

And the Lord was with *Joseph,* and he was a *prosperous* man. (Gen. 39 : 2.)

So the Lord *blessed the latter end of Job* more than the beginning. (Job. 42 : 12.)

WORLDLY **MISERY AND DESTITUTION** THE LOT OF THE GODLY.

They were *stoned,* they were *sawn asunder,* were *tempted,* were *slain* with the *sword;* they wandered about in sheepskins and goat-skins; being *destitute, afflicted, tormented;* . . . they wandered in *deserts,* and in *mountains,* and in *dens* and *caves* of the earth. (Heb. 11 : 37, 38.)

These are they which came out of *great tribulation.* (Rev. 7 : 14.)

Yea, and all that will live godly in Christ Jesus shall *suffer persecution.* (2 Tim. 3 : 12.)

And ye shall be *hated of all men* for my name's sake. (Luke 21 : 17.)

126.

WORLDLY PROSPERITY A REWARD OF RIGHTEOUSNESS AND A BLESSING.

There is no man that hath left house, or brethren, or sisters, or father, or mother, or wife, or children, or lands, for my sake and the gospel's, but he shall receive a *hundred fold now in this time, houses,* and brethren, and sisters, and mothers, and children, and *lands.* (Mark 10 : 29, 30.)

I have been young, and now am old; yet have I *not seen the righteous forsaken nor his seed begging bread.* (Ps. 37 : 25.)

Blessed is the man that feareth the Lord. . . . *Wealth* and *riches* shall be in his *house.* (Ps. 112 : 1, 3.)

If thou return unto the Almighty, thou shalt be built up. . . . Then shalt thou *lay up gold* as dust. (Job. 22 : 23, 24.)

In the house of the righteous is *much treasure.* (Prov. 15 : 6.)

WORLDLY PROSPERITY A CURSE AND A BAR TO FUTURE REWARD.

Blessed be ye *poor.* (Luke 6 : 20.)

Lay not up for yourselves treasures *upon earth.* . . . For where your treasure is there will your heart be also. (Matt. 6 : 19, 21.)

And it came to pass that the *beggar died,* and was carried by the angels into *Abraham's bosom.* (Luke 16 : 22.)

It is easier for a camel to go through the eye of a needle, than for a *rich* man to *enter into the kingdom of God.* (Matt. 19 : 24.)

Woe unto you that are *rich!* for ye have received your consolation. (Luke 6 : 24.)

127.

THE CHRISTIAN YOKE IS EASY.

Come unto me all ye that labor and are heavy laden and I will give you *rest*. Take my yoke upon you. . . . For *my yoke is easy and my burden is light*. (Matt. 11 : 28, 29, 30.)

THE CHRISTIAN YOKE IS **NOT** EASY.

In the world ye *shall have tribulation*. (John 16 : 33.)
Yea, and ALL that will live godly in Christ Jesus shall suffer *persecution*. (2 Tim. 3 : 12.)
Whom the Lord loveth he *chasteneth*, and *scourgeth* every son whom he receiveth . . . . For if ye be *without* chastisement then are ye *bastards* and not sons. (Heb. 12 : 6, 8.)

128.

THE FRUIT OF GOD'S SPIRIT IS LOVE AND GENTLENESS.

The fruit of the spirit is *love, peace, joy, gentleness,* and *goodness*. (Gal. 5 : 22.)

THE FRUIT OF GOD'S SPIRIT IS **VENGEANCE** AND **FURY**.

And the spirit of the Lord came upon him and he *slew a thousand men*. (Judg. 15 : 14.)
And it came to pass on the morrow that the evil spirit *from God* came upon Saul . . . and there was a javelin in Saul's hand. And Saul *cast the javelin;* for he said, I will *smite David* even to the wall with it. (1 Sam. 18 : 10, 11.)

129.

LONGEVITY ENJOYED BY THE WICKED.

Wherefore do the wicked live, *become old,* yea, are mighty in power? Their *seed* is established *in their sight with them, and their offspring before their eyes.* (Job 21 : 7, 8.)

They [men of the world] are *full of children* and leave the rest of their substance to their babes. (Ps. 17 : 14.)

Though a sinner do evil a hundred times and his *days be prolonged,* yet surely I know that it shall be well with them that fear God. (Eccl. 8 : 12.)

But the sinner being *a hundred years old* shall be accursed. (Is. 65 : 20.)

LONGEVITY **DENIED** TO THE WICKED.

But it shall not be well with the wicked, *neither shall he prolong his days.* (Eccl. 8 : 13.)

Bloody and deceitful men *shall not live out half their days.* (Ps. 55 : 23.)

The *years* of the wicked shall be *shortened.* (Prov. 10 : 27.)

They [the hypocrites] *die in youth.* (Job 36 : 14.)

Be not over much wicked, neither be foolish; why shouldst thou *die before thy time?* (Eccl. 7 : 17.)

130.

POVERTY IS A BLESSING.

Blessed be ye *poor.* . . . *Woe* unto you that are *rich!* (Luke 6 : 20, 24.)

Hath not God chosen the *poor* of this world, rich in faith, and *heirs of the kingdom?* (James 2 : 5.)

RICHES A BLESSING.

The rich man's *wealth* is his *strong tower,* but the destruction of the poor is their poverty. (Prov. 10 : 15.)

If thou return unto the Almighty then thou shall be *built up.* . . . Thou shalt then *lay up gold* as dust. (Job 22 : 23, 24.)

And the Lord blessed the latter end of Job more than the beginning, for he had 14,000 sheep, and 6,000 camels, and a *thousand* yoke of oxen, and *a thousand* she asses. (Job 42 : 12.)

NEITHER POVERTY NOR RICHES A BLESSING.

Give me *neither poverty nor riches;* feed me with food convenient for me; lest I be full, and deny thee and say, Who is the Lord? or lest I be *poor and steal,* and take the name of my God in vain. (Prov. 30 : 8, 9.)

131.

WISDOM A SOURCE OF ENJOYMENT.

Happy is the man that findeth *wisdom.* . . . Wisdom's ways are ways of *pleasantness and all her paths are peace.* (Prov. 3 : 13, 17.)

WISDOM A SOURCE OF VEXATION, GRIEF, AND SORROW.

And I gave my heart to know wisdom. . . . I perceived that this also was *vexation* of spirit. For in much wisdom is *much grief,* and he that increaseth knowledge, *increaseth sorrow.* (Eccl. 1 : 17, 18.)

132.

A GOOD NAME A BLESSING.

A good name is *better than precious ointment.* (Eccl. 7 : 1.)

A good name is rather to be chosen than *great riches.* (Prov. 22 : 1.)

A GOOD NAME IS A **CURSE.**

Woe unto you when all men shall *speak well* of you. (Luke 6 : 26.)

133.

LAUGHTER COMMENDED.

To everything there is a season, and a time. . . . A time to weep, and a time to *laugh.* (Eccl. 3 : 1, 4.)

Then I *commended mirth,* because a man hath *no better thing* under the sun than to eat, and to drink, and to be *merry.* (Eccl. 8 : 15.)

LAUGHTER **CONDEMNED.**

Woe unto you that laugh now. (Luke 6 : 25.)

Sorrow is better than laughter; for by the sadness of the countenance the heart is made better. The heart of the *wise* is in the house of *mourning;* but the heart of the *fool* is in the house of *mirth.* (Eccl. 7 : 3, 4.)

134.

THE ROD OF CORRECTION A REMEDY FOR FOOLISHNESS.

Foolishness is bound in the heart of a child, but the rod of correction will *drive it far from him.* (Prov. 22 : 15.)

THERE IS **NO** REMEDY FOR FOOLISHNESS.

Though thou shouldest *bray a fool in a mortar,* . . . yet will *not* his foolishness depart from him. (Prov. 27 : 22.)

135.

A FOOL SHOULD BE ANSWERED ACCORDING TO HIS FOLLY.

Answer a fool according to his folly. (Prov. 26 : 5.)

A FOOL SHOULD **NOT** BE ANSWERED ACCORDING TO HIS FOLLY.

Answer *not* a fool according to his folly. (Prov. 26 : 4.)

136.

TEMPTATION TO BE DESIRED.

My brethren, I count it all *joy* when ye fall into *temptation.* (James 1 : 2.)

TEMPTATION **NOT** TO BE DESIRED.

Lead us *not* into temptation. (Matt. 6 : 13.)

137.

PROPHECY IS SURE.

We have also a more *sure word of prophecy,* whereunto we do well that we take heed, as unto a *light* that shineth in a dark place. (2 Pet. 1 : 19.)

PROPHECY IS **NOT** SURE.

At what instant I shall *speak* concerning a nation, and concerning a kingdom, to pluck up, and to pull down, and to destroy it; if that nation against whom I have pronounced turn from their evil, I will *repent* of the evil that I thought to do unto them. And at what instant I shall speak concerning a nation and concerning a kingdom, to build and to plant it; if it do evil in my sight, that it obey not my voice, then I will *repent* of the good wherewith I *said I would* benefit them. (Jer. 18 : 7-10.)

138.

MAN'S LIFE WAS TO BE
ONE HUNDRED AND TWENTY YEARS.

His days shall be a hundred and twenty years. (Gen. 6 : 3.)

MAN'S LIFE IS BUT **SEVENTY** YEARS.

The days of our years are three score years and ten. (Ps. 90 : 10.)

139.

THE FEAR OF MAN WAS TO BE UPON EVERY BEAST.

The *fear* of you and the *dread* of you shall be on *every beast* of the earth. (Gen. 9 : 2.)

THE FEAR OF MAN IS **NOT** UPON THE LION.

A *lion* turneth not away for *any.* (Prov. 30 : 30.)

140.

MIRACLES A PROOF OF DIVINE MISSION.

Now when John had heard in the prison the works of Christ, he sent two of his disciples, and said unto him, Art thou he that should come, or do we look for another? Jesus answered and said unto them, Go and show John again those things which ye do hear and see; the *blind* receive their *sight,* and the *lame walk,* the *lepers* are *cleansed,* and the *deaf hear,* the *dead are raised.* (Matt. 11 : 2-5.)

Rabbi, we know that thou art a teacher come from God; for *no man can do these miracles* that thou doest *except God be with him.* (John 3 : 2.)

And Israel saw that *great work* which the Lord done upon the Egyptians; and the people feared the Lord and believed the Lord and *his servant Moses.* (ex. 14 : 31.)

141.

MIRACLES **NOT** A PROOF OF DIVINE MISSION.

And Aaron cast down his rod before Pharaoh, and before his servants, and it became a serpent. Then Pharaoh also called the wise men and the sorcerers; now the magicians of Egypt, *they also did in like manner* with their enchantments, for they cast down every man his rod, and *they became serpents.* (Ex. 7 : 10-12.)

If there arise among you a prophet, or a dreamer of dreams, and giveth thee a *sign* or a *wonder,* and the sign or the wonder *come to pass* wherein he spake unto thee, saying, Let us go after other gods which thou hast not known, and let us serve them, thou *shalt not hearken* unto the words of that *prophet* or that dreamer of dreams. (Deut. 13 : 1-3.)

If I by Beelzebub *cast out devils,* by whom do your *sons* cast them out? (Luke 11 : 19.)

142.

MOSES WAS A VERY MEEK MAN.

Now, the man Moses, was *very meek,* above all the men that were upon the face of the earth. (Num. 12 : 3.)

MOSES WAS A VERY **CRUEL** MAN.

And Moses said unto them, Have ye saved all the women alive? . . . Now, therefore, *kill every male* among the *little ones,* and *kill every woman* that hath known a man. (Num. 31 : 15, 17.)

143.

ELIJAH WENT UP TO HEAVEN.

And Elijah *went up* by a whirlwind into *heaven.* (2 Kings 2 : 11.)

NONE BUT CHRIST EVER ASCENDED INTO HEAVEN.

No man hath ascended up to heaven but he that came down from heaven, even the Son of Man. (John 3 : 13.)

144.

ALL SCRIPTURE IS INSPIRED.

All scripture is given by *inspiration* of God. (2 Tim. 3 : 16.)

SOME SCRIPTURE IS **NOT** INSPIRED.

But I speak this *by permission and not by commandment.* (1 Cor. 7 : 6.)

But to the rest speak I, *not the Lord.* (1 Cor. 7 : 12.)

That which I speak, I speak it *not after the Lord.* (2 Cor. 11 : 17.)